AF440058

*"All that we are is story.
It is what we arrive with.
It is all we leave behind.
We are story. All of us.
When we take the time to share those stories with each
other, we get bigger inside, we see each other, we
recognize our kinship, we change the world, one story at
a time."
- Richard Wagamese*

*I dedicate this book to the man who encouraged me to
write poems, my grandfather Rasmus Husby.*

*I also dedicate this book to my loving and supporting
family, my husband Gabriel and my children Ofelia,
Cornelius and Julius. I love you!*

*And finally, I dedicated this book to all of you
who have ever felt powerless, because someone
took advantage of your body and soul. It is your
time now, to spread your wings, take back your
power and know the truth of who you are.*

A COLLECTION OF POEMS OVER 25 YEARS

12 YEARS OLD

1.

Dear golden diary,

I am twelve years old and he has given me a beer.
I am drunk

He touched my breasts and made me watch porn
It was disgusting.
I threw up.

I will never drink beer again.

12 - 21 YEARS

2.

Little girl, Never more

Brother, what is happening
Do not come
Do not go
Sister, can you see me?
Worries, never peace
Perfect? no
Scared? yes

Little girl,
Never more

3.

Go away!
Do not talk to me!
I want to sleep now
It is dark
Teddy come,
Let us dream the night away.

4.

When tiredness awakens
And all happiness goes to bed
Then you can only sleep
And wait for the night again

5.

The hidden truths of the past wait by the door.
Why don't you let them come in?

The past needs a passage.

If you don't let it in, you can not come out.

You tried to forget.
The truth never forgets.
It will stay at your door forever.

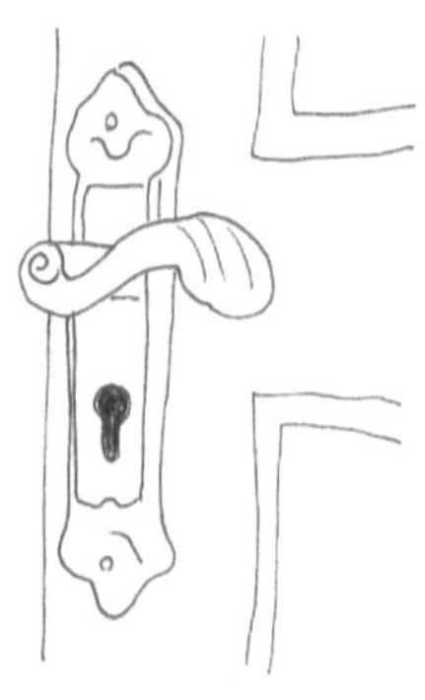

6.

Delicious drinks
Sleepless nights
You stand still
In your dark corner

Speaking voices
You swallow

Live
In your corner in the light

Just a small step
And you are there
Back
In your dark corner

7.

Grey
Paper
Empty
Filled with letters
Screaming
Give me life!

Empty
Paper
Grey

8.

Wandering around with anx-
iety
in a garden
Where only weeds grow

In a small glade you can
almost see
a withered forget-me-not

Once pure and beautiful
Then came anxiety
When?
No one knows
Nor if it will be forgotten

On that day
The garden will be filled with
flowers of all colors
Even forget-me-nots will be there

In memory
Of the anxiety
That was once mine

9.

I can fly far away
High up there
Hovering over the others
In between the clouds I fly
Hiding
Forgetting

And when the loss gets to big
You will find me

Dangling with my legs from the moon.

10.

Deep the treasure was lying
Undisturbed on the bottom of the ocean
Trapped in a mussel shell
Maybe it is time now,
To let it be free?

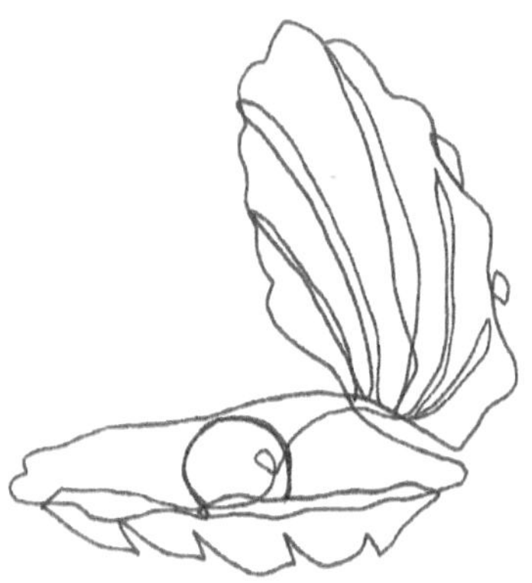

26- 29 YEARS

11.

If the sky falls down on your head
If all the rivers of the world are flooded
If the sun's ray sets the earth on fire

As long as you live
It will never be too late
To let the song of your souls sing
To be whole

12.

There is a longing
in those of us
Who just manage to listen
In us it will be free,
But never disappear
In us who never dare to
Free it from its prison

In those of us
Who just manage to listen

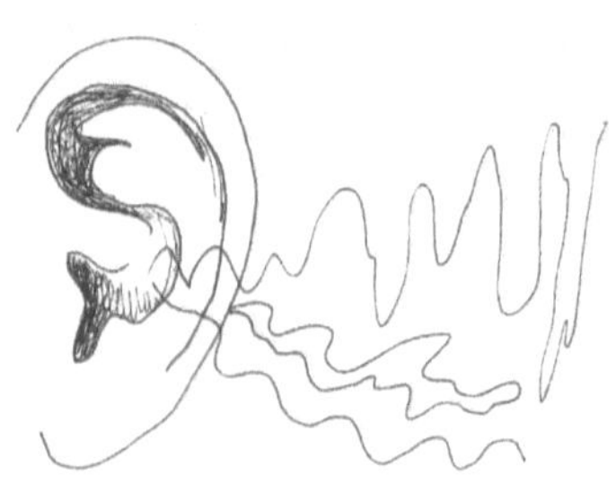

13.

An anxiety for the darkness
Has robbed the joy of life
Oh you scared little friend
can you see the light in the dark?

In it
you will start your life

14.

The beauty of a butterfly
Is hidden in the cocoon
On the day of revelation
Everyone will see
How beautiful it is

15.

Can you imagine how easy it is
To make a burning flame go out?

How easy it is
To forget the beaming self?

But even little gravel grains are filled with this energy
That can neither arise or disappear.

16.

Sick?
I was not, right?
That was just something they told me
That I was
Sick

17.

What times are these
That make us not
Keep up with time?

What we not keep up
Is that more important
Than the time we kept up?

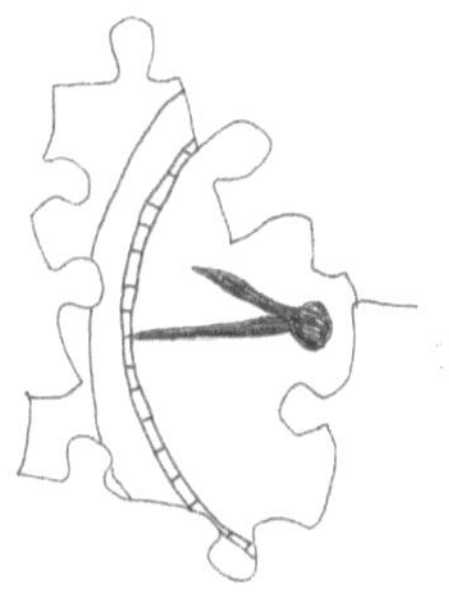

18.
There was a time when I wrote to survive
Poem after poem
I needed the words
To see all my emotions on paper.
Page by page
Words of sadness.
The more misery. The more healing.

There was a longing
For a new time.
When what I wrote,
Could make others survive.
But how can you help others,
When you are about to drown yourself?

There is a time.
That time is now.
When I no longer feel like writing to survive.
Nor for other survival.

I want to write unconditionally.
Because writing is a thing of its own.
A part of creation.
A piece of the puzzle of my time.

29- 32 YEARS

19.

So it was not in the light
You would find the way
Back to your heart
But in the dawn
Between day and night.

20.

In the darkness of the dawn
I opened the door
To the house
Where the time stood still

So quiet
Oh so quiet
So alone and sad

No one to witness
of the life once lived
Of the dance and the joy
Of the sadness and cry
Of the emotions and life
of the people

A house without people
Just walls and roof
Just the shell of all
that is was

Without people
No life
Without people
No style

Soon
Oh so soon
Dear house

will you be more than a house
No longer just a shell

Soon we will march right in
over the doorstep
and give you back
Your glow and your grace

And you give us your protection
And with gratefulness we thank you
Because we both
are in need of each other.

21.

There is a fire inside
That can not be tamed
When injustice and cruelty takes place
The flames burns even stronger
By the truth
Ready to burn right through it
So that from the ashes
a new
and better world
can arise.

22.

Far ahead you will find me
Before the rest of them
The one that found the path
The one that got there first
And the right fuel I was sent there
Fast I travelled
Like really fast
As if I cracked the code
Before the rest of them

Far ahead of the others
The others are there behind
Only me here in the front

It is so beautiful
But only me to see it
I try to tell them
So that they to can get here!

Some are on their way
Others are fine where they are

Far ahead you will find me
I will wait for you
Sometimes I will even wander back
Trying to walk with you
But I can not move your feets
Only you can
If you want to

Sometimes it gets lonely
Being where no one is
I could miss a friend
Who have walked the same path
One that knows the price
Of walking ahead of the rest
One that knows the fires you have fought
The rivers you had to swim over
The mountains you have climbed
And all the winds that tried to blow you over.

On the days when a lot of people come together
To celebrate the sun
It gets really clear
I am the only adult over here
Together with the most precious creatures of the earth
The children with the diamond eyes
And the true fire
Burning in their hearts

But they never walked the same path as me
Their journey starts now

And I will run with them for as far as I cope
I hope they will not finish alone
But wander over the finish line
Together
Far far ahead.

23.

Allow me to be sad for a little while
I promise to get back up again
To shine again
as the warm rays of the sun

But right now
In this moment
I just want to cry
Feel the sadness and the pain
Its realness
And not be pretending

So please give me this moment
To be sad with myself

I promise to rise
Again.

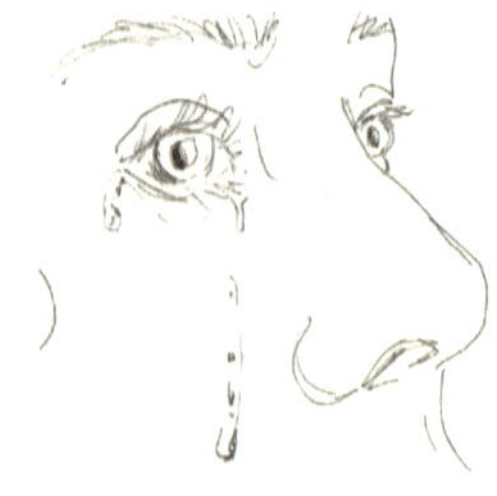

24.

When sadness
Came out as text
It was
No longer left
In the heart.

25.

This place fills me
Of moments
Of 100%
Presence
In nature
And
In me.

26.

It was never my responsibility
To make you a better person
It was never my responsibility
To carry your responsibility
To hide your crimes
To protect you
From others finding out

It was never my responsibility
To give you love
To care for you
To be your family
When all you could give
Was the physical material

It is my responsibility
To stop taking responsibility
For your responsibility
Because it was never my responsibility
To make you a better person.

27.

I look in the mirror
I do not look like myself anymore
Within
I feel so much younger.

In the mirror I do not see a girl
But a woman
I look down on my body
It doesn't look
like I feel.

- I have not been kind to you,
I say.

-   I have not given you any credit.
Was never satisfied with you.

-   It is not your fault,
You respond.

-   It just happend.

But we both know this,
it is not true,
It happened when someone decided
they had the right to my body

I ran away then.
And I dared not to come back to you.

Then came the transformation
Pulled me back into my shape.

Where I am currently
on a voyage of discovery.

- I Should love you more,
I say.

-   I should take care of you.
But then you answer me.

- See me as I am.

And we both know this now
We are not two pieces
You are me.

32-37 YEARS

28.

I have stopped saving the world
One day it just hit me
It was never the world
who needed to be saved
It was me.

29.

To come home
You sometimes need to travel
The roads you know well
That all off a sudden
With no warnings
Changed its appearance

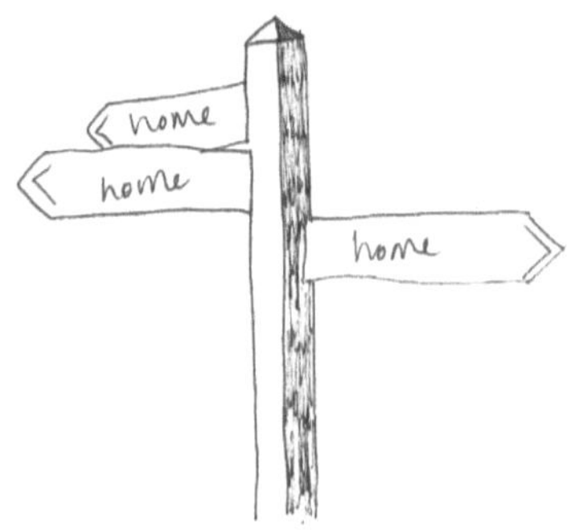

30.

Allow me to be happy
Just let me feel the joy of this moment
And the feeling of it all being perfect
I promise to fight again when needed

But right now
In this moment

I just want to enjoy
and thank life
For all the good that I have.

31.

In that moment
She dried her tears
And rinsed the kale
in cold tapping water

It just hit her

It was never like this
She had imagined
Life to be

And that she would never meet her abuser again.

32.

Freedom
I think it exist in nature
It is where I can feel it the most

I thank it
For finally being free!

33.

One should think
That this is the end

But this is just the beginning

There will be new battles
But when they come
Just spread your wings
And feel the power within your self

It is your time now
To be the one, You where always ment to be.

ABOUT THE AUTHOR

Miriam Husby Stener

Miriam is from Norway but is currently living in Sweden where she works online as a Spiritual coach, Auramediator and a Spiritual practitioner within New Thought. 
This is her first poem-collection and it is based on her own journey from being abused as a child towards claiming her power back, in mind, spirit and body.

If you enjoyed these poems you can follow her on Social Media and let her know in a DM.
Instagram: @miriamstener @miriamhstener @poems_by_miriam
Facebook: Miriam Stener

FREE GIFT!!! As a thank you for buying this poemcollection you can collect your free gift here: https://miriamstener.mykajabi.com/optin-freegift-littlegirlnevermore